PROFIT SHARING

The Chapman Guide to
Making Money an Asset in Your Marriage

GARY D. CHAPMAN, PH.D.

TYNDALE HOUSE PUBLISHERS, INC.

Carol Stream, Illinois

Visit Tyndale's exciting Web site at www.tyndale.com

TYNDALE and Tyndale's quill logo are registered trademarks of Tyndale House Publishers, Inc.

Profit Sharing: The Chapman Guide to Making Money an Asset in Your Marriage

Designed by Ron Kaufmann

Edited by Kathryn S. Olson

Library of Congress Cataloging-in-Publication

Chapman, Gary D., date.
  Profit Sharing : the Chapman guide to making money an asset in your marriage / Gary D. Chapman.
  p. cm.
  Includes bibliographical references and index.
  ISBN-13: 978-1-4143-0016-0 (hc : alk. paper)
  ISBN-10: 1-4143-0016-6 (hc : alk. paper)
  1. Marriage--Religious aspects--Christianity. 2. Money--Religious aspects--Christianity. 3. Finance, Personal--Religious aspects--Christianity.
I. Title. II. Title: Guide to making money an asset in your marriage.
  BV835.C453 2007
  241'.68--dc22   2007006680

Printed in the United States of America

13 12 11 10 09 08 07
7   6   5   4   3   2   1

Table of Contents

Introduction

Could we survive without money? Well, it depends on where you live. My academic background is anthropology, the study of cultures. There are a few primitive cultures in the world where people live without money. The men hunt for meat, while the wives and children work the gardens. Everyone in the village shares the food. When a couple gets married, the men of the village build them a thatched-roof house. Clothing, such as it is, is made from the skins of animals. Thus, the basic needs for food, clothing, and shelter are met without any need for money.

However, if you are reading this book, you do not live in this kind of moneyless society. In the modern industrial world, most couples do not build their own houses, grow their own food, or make their own clothing. We are a society of specialists: Some of us build houses, others make clothing, and others produce and distribute food. We each receive money for the work we perform. With this money, we then buy from others the things we desire. This system of production and distribution is complex, but for the most part, it works fairly well. In the United States, most people manage to obtain food, clothing, and shelter.

Why then is money often the number-one source of conflict in American marriages? The poorest couples in America have abundance compared to the masses of the world's population. I am convinced that the problem does not lie in the amount of money that a couple possess but rather in their attitudes toward money and the manner in which they handle it. The problem is not really money; it is their relationship with money. If they could find a more wholesome perspective on money—that is, change the way they think about money—and find a positive way to handle money, then money would cease to be an area of conflict and would become an asset to their marriage.

This is a book on marriage and money. For over thirty years as a marriage counselor, I have been listening to couples argue about money. Here are some of the complaints I frequently hear:

- "He could get a better job if he would try."

- "She spends more money than we both make, and we both have good jobs."

- "I never know how much money we have because he won't let me see the checkbook."

- "He makes investments that are foolish. He has lost thousands of dollars."

- "Her parents keep giving her money; I don't like that."

- "Why can't we save something? We've been married for ten years and don't even have a savings account."

- "All I ask is that she record the checks that she writes. Balancing our checkbook is a nightmare."

- "He doesn't understand that when you put things on a credit card, eventually you have to pay for them. We're ten thousand dollars in debt, and all we're able to pay each month is the interest."

- "She bought a $300 dress. Do you know how much food $300 would buy?"

- "He pledged $5,000 to the church building fund. I don't know where he thinks that money is going to come from."

- "She keeps telling me that she grew up with a different lifestyle. Well, I'm sorry. I'm not her father. I don't go to work in a shirt and tie every day."

- "He bought a new car and didn't even discuss it with me."

- "How can we afford to invest when we don't have enough money to buy the baby's milk?"

- "She keeps buying lottery tickets. Do you know the chances of ever winning the lottery? It's like throwing our money out the window."

Perhaps you could add a few comments yourself—things you've said or heard your spouse say

regarding money. The purpose of this book is to help the two of you learn to work as a team in obtaining and managing money so that you are working together rather than against each other. Teamwork produces profit sharing. Each of you is a benefactor. Money becomes not a battleground but a means of helping you obtain things that will enhance your marriage.

I have purposefully kept this book short because I know that you are busy. I hope that the brief time you invest in reading the book will produce huge dividends in your marriage.

1

*B*efore we look at the various dynamics related to handling money in marriage, we must first of all put money into its proper perspective. Some couples live as though the accumulation of money and the acquisition of material possessions are the focus of life. These couples live to get. A new purchase brings momentary pleasure. Between acquisitions, they experience emotional lows while anticipating the next moment of pleasure. I don't need to tell you that such an attitude does little to create marital satisfaction.

Jesus lived a rather simple lifestyle, but he impacted human history more than any person who has ever lived. I shall never forget the day I read this statement spoken by Jesus: "A man's life does not consist in the abundance of his possessions."[1] It changed my perspective on money forever. It also resonated with my experience. Hundreds of well-to-do couples have sat in my office over the past thirty years and made statements like this: "We sold our souls for the acquisition of *things*, and now we are bankrupted spiritually and emotionally. We have things . . . but life is empty."

RELATIONSHIPS, NOT THINGS

Real satisfaction is found not in money (any amount of it) but in loving relationships with God, our spouse, our children, and our friends. Loving relationships are our greatest asset. This is most often realized in moments of crisis. Many times I have stood outside the room of a hospital intensive-care center when a child was in critical condition because of an automobile accident or a life-threatening illness. What matters to the parents at that point is not how much money they have or the size of their house, but the friends who come to stand with them in the midst of deep pain. In the experience of physical and emotional crisis, all humankind stands on level ground—some have friends and some do not. Money is no replacement for friendships.

If you believe that more money and more material possessions will bring you marital happiness, you have the wrong attitude. Money can be used to provide more creature comforts, but money will not create a successful marriage. It is righteous living, love, patience, gentleness, and compassion that build meaningful relationships. It is treating each other with dignity, respect, love, and care that creates a happy marriage. This can be attained in the poorest of circumstances as well as in the homes of the affluent. If you are telling yourselves, "We'll be happier when we get more money," you are deceiving yourselves. Some of the happiest couples I know live near the poverty level. I am not saying that they do not aspire for more; they do. But they are under no illusion that more will automatically bring greater happiness.

In fact, quite the opposite can be true. I remember Paul Brown and his wife, Jill, (not their real names) who came to my office, separated and hurting. "We've got it all," Paul said, "and now all of it means nothing. We left God out of our lives; we didn't have time for friends. I worked two jobs. We've got our 4,500-square-foot house; we've got the cars; we've got money in the bank; but in the midst of it all, we've lost each other. I'd give it all away today if we could go back and start over in the little apartment where we lived when we first got married. In those days we had nothing, but we were happy. Today, we have everything, and we're miserable." With a great deal of counseling, Paul and Jill rediscovered each other. They did, in fact, lower their standard of living and raise their level of happiness. However, they could have saved themselves twelve years of miserable affluent living if they had found a proper perspective on money earlier in life.

The desire to have more material possessions is not necessarily an evil desire. The problem comes when we allow money to become the focus of our lives. The Scriptures say, "The love of money is a root of all kinds of evil. Some people, eager for money, have wandered from the faith and pierced

themselves with many griefs."[2] Such sorrows are not the result of having money or not having money, but of *loving* money. When obtaining money becomes the motivating force of our lives, we set ourselves up for "many griefs," such as the loss of marital intimacy. When, on the other hand, we keep money in its proper place, it becomes an asset to the marriage.

JOINT OWNERSHIP

The second aspect of money about which many couples need a change of attitude is the area of ownership. In marriage, it is no longer "my money" and "your money" but rather "our money." In the same manner, it is no longer "my debts" or "your debts" but rather "our debts." If, before you marry, one of you owes $5,000 on an educational loan and the other owes $50 to a local department store, after the wedding you are collectively in debt $5,050. When you accept each other as partners, you accept each other's liabilities as well as each other's assets.

That is the reason full disclosure of assets and liabilities should be made by both partners before marriage. It is not wrong to enter marriage with debts, but you ought to discuss those debts beforehand and agree upon a plan and schedule of repayment. Most couples have some debts when they come to marriage, and a full disclosure by each will help them to face marriage realistically.

I have known couples who failed to discuss this area sufficiently before marriage and realize after the wedding that together they have a debt so large that they already feel a financial noose around their necks. What a tragedy to begin marriage with such a handicap. In my opinion, a large debt without a realistic means of repayment is sufficient cause to postpone the wedding.

In the same way, your assets are now joint assets. She may have $6,000 in a savings account and he may have only $90, but when they marry, *they* have $6,090. If you do not feel comfortable with this oneness, then you are not ready for marriage. The very motif of marriage is unity, oneness, togetherness. When it comes to finances, you must move toward unity.

There may be cases in which, because of very large estates or children from a previous marriage, the couple would be wise to retain individual ownership of certain properties or assets. But for most of us, the principle of unity implies joint savings accounts, checking accounts, property ownership, and so on. We are now a team, and we want to express our unity in finances as well as in other areas of life. Since it is *our* money, it means that neither of us will try to control the finances. Instead, we will manage our finances together as a team, using the best of our past experience and wisdom.

Certainly, one spouse may regularly write the checks for the monthly bills and balance the checkbook, but the other partner needs to have full access to all financial matters and freedom to express opinions and negotiate decisions. When one partner tries to control the finances to the exclusion of the other, that person becomes a parent, and the partner, a child. One wife said, "I am ashamed to say this, but it illustrates the problem: Every time I need a pair of hose, I have to go to my husband and say, 'May I have five dollars to buy a pair of hose?' It's horrible. I feel like a child." Such an arrangement does not strengthen the marital relationship and will inevitably result in numerous conflicts.

If you and your spouse embrace the two realities discussed in this chapter—(1) our relationship is more important than the amount of money we have, and (2) whatever we possess belongs to us jointly—then you will have laid the foundation for making money an asset in your marriage.

PUTTING THE PRINCIPLES INTO PRACTICE

1. In the past, what has been your attitude toward money? What changes do you need to make in your attitude?

2. Are you willing to embrace the concept that your marriage is more important than the accumulation of money and material possessions? Would you be willing to verbalize this to your spouse?

3. Are you willing to embrace the idea that all your money and possessions now belong to

both of you equally and that all your debts are now "our debts"? Would you be willing to verbalize this to your spouse?

4. As an act of affirming these attitudes, perhaps the two of you would like to sign and date the following statement:

We recognize that money will never bring us happiness, that our relationship to each other is more important than what we possess. We further agree that all our possessions belong to us jointly and that all our debts are shared. We will work as a team to manage our finances in such a way as to enhance our relationship.

_____

Husband   Date

_____

Wife   Date

2

$\mathscr{W}$ork is introduced in the first chapter of the Bible. God said to Adam and Eve, "Be fruitful and increase in number; fill the earth and subdue it. Rule over the fish of the sea and the birds of the air and over every living creature that moves on the ground."[1] Not only were they to have children, but they were to work in order to provide for those children. In the second chapter of the book of Genesis, we get a clearer picture of what that work involved: "The LORD God took the man and put him in the Garden of Eden to work it and take care of it."[2]

Please note that working preceded the Fall. Some have implied that work was a part of the

Curse after Adam and Eve sinned. This was not the case; God instituted work before man sinned. Work is a gift of God. When we work, we are cooperating with the divine plan.

God created humans with a mind that had great capacity for learning. But they did not start out knowing all the secrets of the universe. God commanded Adam to *subdue*; that is, to acquire a knowledge and mastery over his material environment and to bring its elements into the service of humankind. Every time I fly in an airplane, I thank God for that mandate. Every time I ride in an automobile, I'm glad someone obeyed God. Every time I turn on a light, I'm glad for someone's work.

To find our work is to find our place in the world. Work is applied effort. It is expending our energy for the sake of accomplishing or achieving something. The opposite of work is not leisure or play, but idleness—not investing ourselves in anything.

Work is normal. When God gave the Ten Commandments, he included the concept of work. "Remember the Sabbath day by keeping it holy. Six days you shall labor and do all your work, but the seventh day is a Sabbath to the LORD your God."[3] The emphasis of the command is on the seventh day for rest and worship, but we must not overlook its relationship to working.

Some of our work results in a paycheck, but some of our work has other rewards. The housework of parents is real work, though it brings in no revenue. The homework of children is real work, though the payoff is not in money.

William Bennett in *The Book of Virtues* lists work as one of the ten great virtues. He says, "Those who have missed the joy of work, of a job well done, have missed something very important."[4] Recently I talked to a man who had lost his job. He said, "I enjoy the freedom, but I miss the satisfaction of accomplishment." He was echoing the ancient Hebrew proverb "A longing fulfilled is sweet to the soul."[5] Theologian Carl Henry once said, "When man loses the sacred significance of work, he soon loses the sacred meaning of time and life."[6]

A SACRED CALLING

For the Christian, work is indeed seen as a sacred calling. The word *vocation* means "calling." Each of us has certain interests and abilities. God expects us to use these for the good of humankind and for his ultimate glory. All good work is seen as service to God and, thus, sacred. It is through work that parents provide for the physical needs of their children. Once this is done, they have the opportunity to meet their emotional and spiritual needs. The apostle Paul said, "If anyone does not provide for his relatives, and especially for his immediate family, he has denied the faith and is worse than an unbeliever."[7] The idea is that those who are walking in fellowship with God will see their work as a sacred responsibility.

We typically say of a person who is unwilling to work that he or she is lazy. Laziness in the Bible is always seen as sinful. In the book of Proverbs, we read, "Go to the ant, you sluggard; consider its ways and be wise! It has no commander, no overseer or ruler, yet it stores its provisions in summer and gathers its food at harvest. How long will you lie there, you sluggard? When will you get up from your sleep? A little sleep, a little slumber, a little folding of the hands to rest—and poverty will come on you like a bandit and scarcity like an armed man."[8]

Another proverb reads, "The sluggard craves and gets nothing, but the desires of the diligent are fully satisfied."[9] In the writings of the apostle Paul, we find an antidote for laziness. He said to the Christians who lived in the city of Thessalonica, "Even when we were with you, we gave you this rule: 'If a man will not work, he shall not eat.' We hear that some among you are idle. They are not busy; they are busybodies. Such people we command and urge in the Lord Jesus Christ to settle down and earn the bread they eat."[10]

A NORMAL PART OF LIFE

If we wish to prepare children for adulthood, then we must teach them this truth: Work is a normal part of life. If we do not work, we do not eat. As children get older, we assign them work responsibilities in keeping with their abilities. We let them know that just as Dad works and Mom works, so children also work. Because we work, we get to eat. If we fail to work, we forfeit the privilege of eating.

There is a simple, yet dramatic, way to teach this lesson: You merely assign your children a job and let them know that if they complete the job, they have the privilege of eating dinner that night. If they do not complete the job, they must miss the meal. You need not coax, scold, or intimidate them to complete the job. You simply assign it and explain the consequences. I have yet to meet a child who will miss more than one meal before learning to work. Of course, you must first of all teach the children how to do whatever you expect them to do. Habits of personal hygiene, helping with the laundry, caring for pets, making beds, helping with meals, and other household chores all require learning.

Parents can show their children how to enjoy doing things that have to be done by working with them, by encouraging and expressing appreciation for their efforts, and by modeling for them their own cheerful example. Tasks can be done cheerfully and with pride—or grudgingly and with rebellion. The manner in which we do them is really up to us. It is a matter of choice. There are no menial jobs, only menial attitudes. If children learn to work cheerfully in the home, parents have taught them one of the major ingredients for being successful adults.

THE FINANCIAL IMPACT OF NONPAYING JOBS

As adults, it is typically our work that brings us income. But do not underestimate the financial impact of nonpaying jobs. The husband or wife who mows the lawn has contributed $30 or more (depending on the size of the lawn) to the family assets. The person who cooks meals, washes clothes, vacuums floors, and cleans commodes is also making a positive impact on the financial well-being of the family. Whether or not we receive a paycheck for it, our work impacts positively the financial assets of the marriage.

The Christian couple who is committed to the work ethic revealed in Scripture understands that they are working not only for the benefit of their marriage and family, but also for God. Paul said, "Whatever you do, work at it with all your heart, as working for the Lord, not for men, since you know that you will receive an inheritance from the Lord as a reward. It is the Lord Christ you are serving."[11]

It is by means of work that we obtain money to provide for our needs and to enrich the lives of others. Whether you and your spouse both work for pay or only one gets paid, you both work for the benefit of the family.

PUTTING THE PRINCIPLES INTO PRACTICE

1. If you are employed for pay, do you sense that the manner in which you are investing your energy is making a contribution to the well-being of others and thus bringing glory to God? If not, would you consider exploring the possibility of changing vocations?

2. If your work does not involve a paycheck, do you recognize the intangible value of what

you are doing—the contribution you are making to your family and to others? Is there anything you would like to change about the way you are investing your life?

3. Do you and your spouse agree that providing for the physical, emotional, and spiritual well-being of your family (which includes the two of you) is a sacred responsibility? If so, are you daily asking for God's wisdom?

4. Does either of you feel that it is time to explore the possibility of changes in your work—who works for pay, how many hours that person will work outside the home each week, who takes care of various nonpaying jobs, etc.? If so, discuss this idea and find a strategy to execute these changes.

3

IN GOD WE TRUST

*W*hen I wrote the title of this chapter, I instinctively reached for my wallet and took out my cash. On the back of the one-dollar bill, I read "In God We Trust." I looked at the five-dollar bill and read "In God We Trust." The same was true of the ten- and twenty-dollar bills. And if I'd had a fifty- and a hundred-dollar bill, they would read the same—"In God We Trust."

No matter how much money we have, it is still "in *God* we trust." To trust in money to give life meaning is to trust in an idol. The Scriptures declare, "Every good and perfect gift is from above, coming down from the Father of the heavenly lights, who does not change like shifting shadows."[1] All that we have or ever expect to obtain is a gift from God. There are no "self-made" men.

C. S. Lewis writes, "One of the dangers of having a lot of money is that you may be quite satisfied with the kinds of happiness money can give and so fail to realise your need for God. If everything seems to come simply by signing checks, you may forget that you are at every moment totally dependent on God."[2]

There are individuals who pride themselves on having accumulated great wealth. They may look at themselves as "self-made," but one small germ or virus can quickly change their perspective. We could accomplish nothing without the help of God. Life itself is a gift from God. It is true that we can take steps to preserve our health, and we can develop the mind that God has given us. And through these efforts we can accomplish much in life, as we discussed in chapter 2. But both our bodies and minds are gifts from God.

MAKE GOD YOUR BUSINESS PARTNER

Why am I talking about God in a book whose topic is money and marriage? It's because we were created to live in union with God. We are at our best when we cooperate with God. Many couples have made foolish financial decisions because they left God out of the process. Those who seek God's wisdom and make financial decisions based on the principles revealed in Scripture will save themselves much heartache.

We accept the challenge of work, but we do not depend on ourselves. We look to God for wisdom as to how to use our abilities in the most productive manner. I remember a young man who said to me, "I had wrestled for weeks with an engineering problem and was unable to come up with a workable solution. Finally, a friend of mine suggested that I pray and ask God to give me an answer. I did, and within thirty minutes, it came to me. I had the solution. So I have decided that God and I make a pretty good team." This young man was reaping the benefits of God's offer: "If any of you lacks wisdom, he should ask God, who gives generously to all without finding fault, and it will be given to him."[3]

R. G. LeTourneau, one of the industrial giants of the last generation, often spoke of the day he made God his business partner. He was floundering and deeply in debt when he realized that he was trying to build a business by his own ingenuity. After making God his partner, he built some of the most effective earthmoving equipment ever built. During World War II, his earthmoving machines became the "secret weapons" of the war. After the war, he received the 10th Annual Award of the National Defense Transportation Association as the person whose "achievement contributed most to the effectiveness of the transportation industry in support of national security."[4]

One of the benefits of trusting in God is that we don't have to worry about money. Jesus made this abundantly clear when he said,

> I tell you, do not worry about your life, what you will eat or drink; or about your body, what you will wear. Is not life more important than food, and the body more important than clothes? Look at the birds of the air; they do not sow or reap or store away in

barns, and yet your heavenly Father feeds them. Are you not much more valuable than they? Who of you by worrying can add a single hour to his life? And why do you worry about clothes? See how the lilies of the field grow. They do not labor or spin. Yet I tell you that not even Solomon in all his splendor was dressed like one of these. If that is how God clothes the grass of the field, which is here today and tomorrow is thrown into the fire, will he not much more clothe you, O you of little faith? So do not worry, saying, "What shall we eat?" or "What shall we drink?" or "What shall we wear?" For the pagans run after all these things, and your heavenly Father knows that you need them. But seek first his kingdom and his righteousness, and all these things will be given to you as well.[5]

God is committed to caring for his children. This does not mean that we are to sit back and expect God to do everything. There is an old German proverb that says, "God gives the birds their food, but he does not throw it into their nests." We are to use the mind and body he has given us, but we are to do it in cooperation with him, looking to him for wisdom so that we can complete what he desires us to accomplish in life. Trusting in God means that we no longer need to live under the burden of self-effort.

With God, we have a partner in business who is committed to our well-being. The apostle Paul made this practical when he said, "Do not be anxious about anything, but in everything, by prayer and petition, with thanksgiving, present your requests to God. And the peace of God, which transcends all understanding, will guard your hearts and your minds in Christ Jesus."[6] It is daily talking with God, seeking his wisdom and guidance, that makes us most productive financially as well as in all other areas of life.

MAKE MONEY YOUR SERVANT, NOT YOUR SECURITY BLANKET

In contrast to God-centered living, there are those who place their trust in money. Money becomes their security blanket. Money, for them, is a sign of success. All their decisions are made in response to the question "What offers the greatest financial advantage?" I remember the husband who said to me, "I moved my family across the country, against the advice of my wife and my friends, in order to make $50,000 more per year. In the new location my teenage daughter got involved in drugs and my college-age son got involved in a cult. I have spent far more than I gained, trying to rescue them. I wish I had listened to my wife."

When we trust in God, we realize that some things are more important than money. For the person who trusts in God, the question is, "How will this decision affect my marriage and family?" (In case you hadn't noticed, we are applying the principle discussed in chapter 1, that relationships are more important than things.)

The wise couple will make money their servant. They will seek to use money for the good of their family and to help others. They will never allow money to be their master, dictating their decisions. Jesus addressed this issue when he said, "No one can serve two masters. Either he will hate the one and love the other, or he will be devoted to the one and despise the other. You cannot serve both God and Money."[7]

Too many couples have followed the wrong god and lived to regret it. I remember the middle-aged, female attorney who said with tears in her eyes, "I recently quit my job. For eighteen years, I invested my life in climbing the corporate ladder. Betty Friedan [one of the founders of the modern feminist movement], told us we could have it all. But she didn't tell us how much it would cost. It cost me my first marriage. Now that I have found another husband who loves me, I will not make the same mistake twice. I have realized that, for me, marriage and family are far more important than position and money."

I am not suggesting that wives who trust in God cannot have jobs outside the home. Many wives have been able to pursue a vocation and maintain a healthy marriage and be a responsible parent. It all depends on the nature of the job, the personality of the individuals involved, and the dynamics of the family relationships. What I am saying is that the decision needs to be based on how the job affects the marriage, the children, and one's relationship and service to God—not merely on the desire for money or prestige.

PROMOTE THE KINGDOM OF GOD WITH YOUR WORK

Another way in which trusting in God affects our financial decisions is in the type of job we pursue. For the Christian, all of life comes under the lordship of Christ. Everything we do should be beneficial to others and promote the Kingdom of God. Some jobs do not meet these criteria. The selling of illegal drugs, the promotion of prostitution, and the whole pornographic industry are obvious examples. But there are also other jobs that may not be worthy of your pursuit. Ask yourself these two questions:

- Is what I am doing in my vocation making a positive impact on people?

- Do I sense when I am at work that I am pleasing God?

If you are trusting in God, you will want to be investing your vocational energy in something more than simply "making money."

There are also couples who hear the call of God to invest their lives in Christian ministry. This calling may lead them to work within the church or other Christian organizations. Almost all these people make the conscious choice to live on less money in order to invest their energies in vocational Christian service. The choice to trust in God rather than money as the source of life's meaning will have huge implications for their marriages.

Other couples who trust in God have been given the privilege of accumulating great wealth. They seek to use it for the benefit of their family and the larger community under the direction of God. Still other couples who trust in God live with meager financial income but sense no lack of satisfaction because they are investing their lives in a manner consistent with God's principles. It is not a matter of how much money we have; it is a matter of where we place our trust.

Joshua, the successor to Moses, gave the people of Israel these instructions as he prepared to lead them into the Promised Land:

> Do not let this Book of the Law depart from your mouth; meditate on it day and night, so that you may be careful to do everything written in it. Then you will be prosperous and successful. Have I not commanded you? Be strong and courageous. Do not be terrified; do not be discouraged, for the Lord your God will be with you wherever you go.[8]

Later, Joshua gave this challenge to the Israelites:

> Choose for yourselves this day whom you will serve, whether the gods your forefathers served beyond the River, or the gods of the Amorites, in whose land you are living. But as for me and my household, we will serve the Lord.[9]

I have never met a couple who regretted trusting in God. But I have met hundreds who have trusted in money—some who are wealthy and some who are not—none of whom found ultimate satisfaction in money. When our trust is in God, we will see money as an instrument to be used for good under his direction. Our greatest desire will be to please God as a good manager of the resources he gives us.

PUTTING THE PRINCIPLES INTO PRACTICE

1. Can you sincerely say, "My greatest satisfaction is in pursuing God, not in pursuing money"? If not, would you be willing to change the direction of your pursuits? If so, why not express that decision in a prayer to God?

2. Do you think your spouse would sincerely agree with the statement "My greatest satisfaction is in pursuing God, not in pursuing money"? If not, perhaps the two of you could read this chapter together and discuss the possibility of redirecting the focus of your life.

3. As you read this chapter, did you discover areas of your life where you need the wisdom

of God? If so, perhaps you would like to make the words of James 1:5 your prayer:

If any of you lacks wisdom, he should ask God, who gives generously to all without finding fault, and it will be given to him.

4

Giving Is an Expression of Gratitude

$\mathcal{T}$here are only three things we can do with money: We can give it away, we can save it, or we can spend it. All three are valid ways of using money. In this chapter, we will look at giving it away. Obviously, we cannot and should not give all our money away. Some must be used to meet the physical needs of our families. But if we give none of it away, we are failing to be grateful for what God has given us.

It is interesting that when God laid down concepts by which ancient Israel was to live, he included the area of giving:

A tithe of everything from the land,
whether grain from the soil or fruit from
the trees, belongs to the LORD; it is holy to
the LORD. . . . The entire tithe of the herd
and flock—every tenth animal that passes
under the shepherd's rod—will be holy to
the LORD. . . . These are the commands the
LORD gave Moses on Mount Sinai for the
Israelites.[1]

God did not simply refer to "giving" as a vague
concept. No, he specified that his people were to
give a tenth of their income. The word *holy* means
"separated." They were to separate one tenth of
their possessions and designate them specifically
for the work of God. This gift was to be channeled
through the Levites, the spiritual leaders of Israel,
and used to meet their needs as well as the needs
of the poor. In addition to the tithe, Israel was also
encouraged to give offerings.

Years later, we discover that God has not
changed his mind about this pattern of giving. In
the last book of the Old Testament, we read,

"Will a man rob God? Yet you rob me. But you ask, 'How do we rob you?' In tithes and offerings. You are under a curse—the whole nation of you—because you are robbing me. Bring the whole tithe into the storehouse, that there may be food in my house. Test me in this," says the LORD Almighty, "and see if I will not throw open the floodgates of heaven and pour out so much blessing that you will not have room enough for it. I will prevent pests from devouring your crops, and the vines in your fields will not cast their fruit," says the LORD Almighty. "Then all the nations will call you blessed, for yours will be a delightful land," says the LORD Almighty.[2]

In this passage, the blessing of God is tied to the faithfulness of Israel in giving a tenth of their income back to God. And the curse of God, the removal of God's blessing, is tied to their failure to give.

ARE WE REQUIRED TO GIVE?

In the New Testament, Jesus endorsed the idea of giving a tenth of one's income, while at the same time pointing out to the religious leaders of his day that such giving is to be accompanied by godly living. Jesus said,

> Woe to you, teachers of the law and Pharisees, you hypocrites! You give a tenth of your spices—mint, dill and cummin. But you have neglected the more important matters of the law—justice, mercy and faithfulness. You should have practiced the latter, without neglecting the former.[3]

Jesus emphasized that giving 10 percent of one's income is to be done not as a religious duty but as an expression of gratitude from one's heart; and along with the gift one should exhibit a concern for justice, mercy, and faithfulness to God.

While the New Testament does not require Christians to give 10 percent of their income, it does stress the concept of giving back to God out of what he has given us. Jesus clearly taught that the blessing of God upon our lives is tied to our spirit of gratitude, expressed in giving. Jesus said, "Give, and it will be given to you. A good measure, pressed down, shaken together and running over, will be poured into your lap. For with the measure you use, it will be measured to you."[4] When we express our gratitude to God by giving back to him out of what he has given to us, Jesus promises that God will give us more. One cannot outgive God.

The apostle Paul reiterates this concept when he says,

> Remember this: Whoever sows sparingly will also reap sparingly, and whoever sows generously will also reap generously. Each man should give what he has decided in his heart to give, not reluctantly or under compulsion, for God loves a cheerful giver. And God is able to make all grace abound to you, so that in all things at all times, having all that you need, you will abound in every good work.[5]

Paul clearly states that we are to give out of a heart of gratitude, not out of a sense of compulsion. He also affirms that, in giving, we do not diminish our resources because God will abundantly supply all that we need.

An ancient Hebrew proverb says, "Honor the LORD with your wealth, with the firstfruits of all your crops; then your barns will be filled to overflowing, and your vats will brim over with new wine."[6] The New Testament affirms this concept. Paul said to the Christians living in Philippi who had sent him money for his ministry, "The gifts you sent . . . are a fragrant offering, an acceptable sacrifice, pleasing to God. And my God will meet all your needs according to his glorious riches in Christ Jesus."[7]

Clearly our giving is important to God. I think that's because it is a true reflection of our gratitude to God and our love for people. The question is not whether we will give. The questions are how much shall we give and to whom shall we give it?

HOW MUCH SHALL WE GIVE?

I have always felt strongly that if God required 10 percent of ancient Israel, then those of us who have experienced his forgiveness and the gift of eternal life through Christ our Lord should give even more than that. I believe that 10 percent of one's income is a good starting point and that this should be given off the top of our regular income. Then as we become aware of special opportunities and needs, we may give additional gifts. In the Old Testament, God expected Israel to give 10 percent and even indicated that it already belonged to him. Why should we think that he would expect less of us?

My challenge to Christian couples has always been to give 10 percent of their income to God and adjust their budget to live on the remaining 90 percent. It may require lowering your standard of living, but in the long run, it will raise the quality of your life. Obviously this means that not every couple give the same amount. We give in proportion to what we receive. If we earn $200 a week, then we give $20. If we earn $500, we give $50. If we earn $5,000, we give $500. Whatever our level of income, such giving is a realistic way to start.

R. G. LeTourneau, whom I mentioned in the last chapter, was so greatly blessed by God that in the latter years of his life he gave 90 percent of his income to God and lived on the remaining 10 percent. He once said, "The question is not how much of my money I give to God, but rather how much of God's money I keep for myself."[8] He had learned the joy of giving.

TO WHOM SHOULD WE GIVE?

In Old Testament days, giving was fairly simple. The gifts were to be brought to the Tabernacle (and later, the Temple) where they would be administered by the Levites and priests.

As Christians, we can follow this precedent by giving our tithes to our church. My personal pattern has always been to give 10 percent to the church I attend and to give additional offerings to other organizations as I am able and feel prompted by God.

Many Christian organizations have been created, some by the church and others by individuals and groups of Christians, to meet a particular need or to explore a particular possibility for the expansion of the Kingdom of God. All these kinds of organizations are worthy of support. The churches with whom I have been associated through the years also give some of the funds they receive to other Christian organizations.

It has always been important for me to remember that I do not give *to* the church, but rather I give *to God through* the church. I do not give *to* Christian organizations, but rather I give *to God through* Christian organizations.

There is also a time to give to individuals who are in need. The apostle John speaks of that when he says, "If anyone has material possessions and sees his brother in need but has no pity on him, how can the love of God be in him? Dear children, let us not love with words or tongue but with actions and in truth."[9] Obviously, one should be conscientious about establishing need and not be taken in by scams. It's also important to determine how best to help an individual in need. Often, it's best not to give cash but to provide food or to pay a utility bill. This is especially true if the person who is in need is addicted to alcohol or drugs. Cash gifts to such a person simply help perpetuate a problem.

Christians who recognize that everything we have is a gift from God express this reality by giving out of what we have received. Such giving is an expression of gratitude. The amount we give and the channels through which we direct our giving will vary, but the attitude is always the same: "Thank you, Father, for your goodness to us."

PUTTING THE PRINCIPLES INTO PRACTICE

1. On a scale of one to ten, how grateful are you for what God has given you? Does the level of your giving reflect the level of your gratitude?

2. Are you satisfied with your present pattern of giving? If not, what would you like to see changed?

3. Discuss with your spouse the changes the two of you would like to make in your pattern of giving. (Perhaps your spouse would be willing to read this chapter before you talk about it together.)

5

SAVING IS A SIGN OF WISDOM

$\mathcal{T}$he couple who save a percentage of their income regularly will not only have the reserve funds they need for emergencies but will also have the satisfaction that comes from being good managers of their money. Regular savings ought to be a part of your financial plan.

Some feel that Christians should not save, that saving money is a sign they are not trusting God to provide for the future. However, this is not the perspective found in Scripture, which indicates that we are to be good managers of our money. The wise manager faces the future realistically. A

Hebrew proverb says, "A prudent man foresees the difficulties ahead and prepares for them; the simpleton goes blindly on and suffers the consequences."[1] It is wise to plan ahead to meet the needs of your family, business, or other endeavors.

There are many reasons for saving money. One is illustrated by this story that Jesus told: "Suppose one of you wants to build a tower. Will he not first sit down and estimate the cost to see if he has enough money to complete it? For if he lays the foundation and is not able to finish it, everyone who sees it will ridicule him, saying, 'This fellow began to build and was not able to finish.'"[2] Many couples have plans to build or buy a house in the future. Others have plans for starting a business. Saving money in order to accomplish these objectives is clearly a wise use of money.

You and your spouse will need to agree on the percentage you would like to save, but you should save something on a regular basis. Many financial advisors suggest allotting 10 percent of your net income to savings. You may choose more or less; the choice is yours. However, if you save only what is left over at the end of the week or the month, you will not save. Being *regular* and *consistent* in what you save is more important than the amount you save.

PREPARING FOR THE FUTURE

One of the best reasons to save is the very real possibility of difficult times in the future. Saving is a way of preparing for those difficult times. In the history of Israel, this is illustrated by Joseph, who was called from prison to interpret the dreams of Pharaoh, king of Egypt. The dreams, which God enabled Joseph to interpret, meant that there would be seven years of plenty, followed by seven years of famine. Joseph's financial plan, obviously guided by God, was "to take a fifth of the harvest of Egypt during the seven years of abundance. They should collect all the food of these good years that are coming and store up the grain under the authority of Pharaoh, to be kept in the cities for food. This food should be held in reserve for the country, to be used during the seven years of famine that will come upon Egypt, so that the country may not be ruined by the famine."[3] Pharaoh liked the plan and appointed Joseph to administer it. As a result, Joseph was used of God both to preserve the lives of the citizens of Egypt and also to care for his own family.

Most of us do not have dreams about future difficulties, but we have lived long enough to know that life is not a smooth journey. Difficulties are a part of most of our lives. People lose jobs, get sick, and have disabling accidents. Setting aside some money to prepare for these realities is wise. Again, the wisdom literature says, "In the house of the wise are stores of choice food and oil, but a foolish man devours all he has."[4] In an agricultural economy, people store food and oil. In an industrial economy, people save money so they can buy food and oil.

The Hebrew proverbs offer an illustration from nature: "Go to the ant, you sluggard; consider its ways and be wise! It has no commander, no overseer or ruler, yet it stores its provisions in summer and gathers its food at harvest."[5] There is an old adage that says, "The time to save money is when you have some."

Unfortunately, ours is a consumer society. Many of us have not been taught to save. For every television ad encouraging us to save for the future, there are fifty encouraging us to spend. One young student was asked by his math teacher, "If your father saved ten dollars a week for a whole year, what would he have?" The student replied, "An iPod, a new suit, and a lot of furniture." This was not the answer the teacher was expecting, but it clearly was the mind-set of the student and his father.

SAVING AND INVESTING

There is a difference between saving and investing. The difference lies not only in the level of risk and return on one's money but also in the purpose. Typically, we *save* for an anticipated purpose. We may save for the college education of our children, for the purchase of a new car or house, for Christmas spending, or scores of other anticipated expenditures. We may even save in order to have money to invest. On the other hand, *investing* typically involves funds that are not presently needed or are not designated for a particular purchase in the future. They are set aside, perhaps for retirement or for the purpose of letting the money earn dividends and potentially increase in value.

The typical venues used for savings are bank savings accounts, which have a rather low rate of interest return, and certificates of deposit, which have a somewhat higher rate of return. Investments typically involve the purchase of stocks and bonds, often in the form of mutual funds, which have the potential of bringing in a much higher rate of return but also run the risk of decreasing in value.

Most couples should have considerable money in savings before they begin investing. In today's climate, which encourages not only traditional investing but online investing, many young couples jump into the investment world knowing little about the risks and end up losing far more money than they make. Often they lose money that in their minds was designated for savings. Thus, they undermine their original purpose by the allurement of higher returns.

Establishing a regular pattern of saving is the first step in getting ready to invest. While you are saving, you can educate yourself on the potential and the risks of investing.

If you give 10 percent to God and save 10 percent, that leaves 80 percent to be divided among mortgage payments (or rent), electricity, telephone, heat, water, insurance, furniture, food, medicines, clothes, transportation, education, recreation, and so forth. In the next chapter, we will look at some creative ways of spending that have the potential of freeing up additional funds for saving or giving.

PUTTING THE PRINCIPLES INTO PRACTICE

1. What percentage of your present income are you putting into savings or investments? Are you pleased with this percentage? What changes would you like to make?

2. Would your spouse be willing to join you in a discussion about your present saving and investment plans? Would the two of you profit from reading a basic book on the fundamentals of saving and investing? If so, see the resource section of this book for suggestions.

3. Starting where you are, can the two of you
   agree on the next step you want to take to
   strengthen your program of saving and/or
   investing?

6

A number of years ago, I took a group of college students to Chiapas, the southernmost state of
Mexico, for a visit to the Wycliffe Bible Translators
"jungle camp." Here we observed missionaries being trained in the technique of living in primitive
conditions. They learned how to build houses, ovens,
chairs, beds—all out of materials available in the jungle. I have reflected on that experience many times.
If that same creativity could be used by the average
couple in America, what could be accomplished?

People are instinctively creators. The museums
of art and industry located across the world bear

visual witness to human creativity. We are made in the image of a God who creates, and we who bear his image have tremendous creative potential. The couple who will exercise this creativity in financial matters will find significant assets. Sewing, refinishing used furniture, recycling others' discards, and painting your own house can do wonders for your budget.

In this chapter, I want to challenge you to apply your creativity to the manner in which you spend your money. When I was growing up, my father often said, "A dollar saved is a dollar earned." He was not using that adage to encourage me to put a dollar in the bank; he was encouraging me to compare prices before I bought something. If I could buy the same item for a dollar less in the store next door, I had saved a dollar, which was just as significant as working to earn a dollar. Dad was teaching me to *shop*, not simply *buy*.

Taking the time to compare prices goes against the grain of many men. "I don't want to spend half a day shopping. I want to go in a store, buy what I want, and get out" is their philosophy. If a man has unlimited resources, then that philosophy is feasible. But if finances are tight, that philosophy is irresponsible, is a disservice to his wife, and will likely lead to conflicts in the marriage.

I believe that creative spending could radically change the climate of your marriage. I present the following ideas in an effort to stimulate your creativity about how to get more for your dollar.

This chapter is not written for the wealthy. In fact, the person who has unlimited resources is probably not reading this book. This chapter is for the couple who have average or modest income but who constantly struggle with having enough money to meet the needs of the family.

DISCOUNT SHOPPING

In most towns, there is a good store that sells items cheaper than all the rest. Why not buy your groceries there? Typically, these discount stores, whether they are called that or not, will save you money. If you regularly buy at these stores, you will save several hundred dollars per year on regular household purchases. This is especially true for food and household items. And if you want to save even more, look for the weekly discounts in these discount stores. Stock up on items when they are super discounted.

A second level of discount shopping is using manufacturer's coupons. These are often received in the mail, available in the local newspapers, and sometimes available at the coupon desk or bulletin board in the local store. These coupons can reduce the price of your purchases by several dollars. One lady shared, "I got sixty dollars' worth of groceries for thirty-five dollars after cashing in my coupons." I could tell she was excited about the way her creative spending was impacting the family budget.

Buying at the cheapest store, using coupons, and stocking up on the special sale items can save literally hundreds of dollars on your food and household budget.

RECYCLE SHOPPING

Most communities have Goodwill stores, thrift stores, and Salvation Army stores. These stores serve a valuable purpose in the community. They take discarded items from individuals and then sort and keep only those that are truly usable. They display and sell these items at greatly reduced prices and use the proceeds to minister to those in need.

One customer said, "I started buying clothes for my children here but soon realized that the store had really nice clothes for ladies. I can't believe the money I've saved on my clothes since I started shopping at Goodwill." The added value of shopping at resale stores run by charitable organizations is that you are also helping them fulfill their mission. If you think it is below your dignity to shop at such stores, you probably haven't visited one in a few years. Most of them are well-managed; the clothes and products are clean and in excellent condition.

At one of my marriage seminars, a couple told me that they had saved thousands of dollars by recycle shopping. It all started with an experiment. They agreed that for six months they would seek to buy all their household items, all their clothes, and all the children's toys and school supplies at resale or consignment shops. After the six-month trial period, they were hooked.

FREE SHOPPING

A couple who live in Florida told me they had found something even better than shopping at Goodwill. "We call it *free shopping*," the husband said.

"How does that work?" I asked.

"Three ways," he said. "First, we drive through affluent neighborhoods the night before the discards are to be collected. It's amazing the things you find sitting beside a garbage can. Recently, we found a perfectly good basketball goal. We brought it home, and our kids love it. At first, we felt guilty that maybe we were stealing. So now, we ring the doorbell and ask the family if they would mind our having whatever is sitting beside their garbage can. We've never had anyone refuse to give it to us.

"The second approach is that we have let all our friends know that we are open to receiving hand-me-downs, especially children's clothing and toys. We get more than we need, so we pass the extra items along to others.

"The third approach is to inform our parents of specific toys that our children have requested.

We know that they are going to give the children presents on their birthdays, Christmas, and other occasions, so why not have them purchase things that the children really want?

"With these three approaches, about the only thing we have to buy our children is food. And now that the children are older, next summer we are going to start a garden," he said with a smile.

SEASONAL SHOPPING

Another approach to saving money is seasonal shopping. My wife is an expert in this kind of shopping, which is especially helpful when buying clothing. Karolyn likes to wear nice clothes, and I like to see her in nice clothes. But she never pays full price for anything. She always shops at the seasonal sales. I don't mean the first day of the sale; I mean after it has been reduced one, two, or three times. The other day she came home with a $399 outfit that she had bought for $59. I love the woman, and I love her skills. I told her, "We could not afford for you to work outside the home because you wouldn't have time to save us all this money." I was teasing, but actually, the money she saves by seasonal shopping provides a rather good income.

Even those couples who are not financially strapped have found that seasonal shopping is wise stewardship. All stores have seasonal sales in which products are greatly reduced. The stores want to get rid of their stock so they can bring in the next season's wares. In order to do this, they sell at greatly reduced prices. This is true for large items like cars as well as smaller items like clothes. Seasonal shopping is creative spending, and the profit sharing is great.

Creative spending can become an exciting part of life for the couple who are trying to take hold of their finances, utilize their assets in the best possible manner, and create money that can be used in other ways to enrich their marriage. Another way to use your creativity in helping the family budget is in developing your skills in such crafts as sewing, refinishing furniture, making dolls and stuffed animals. Whatever you make or refurbish almost always costs considerably less than purchasing those items made by someone else. When you allow your children to join you in these creative arts, you have the added advantage of teaching your children the joy of creativity.

I remember the couple who said, "When we got serious about our finances, we set aside a weekly amount to be used to purchase our food. Whatever we didn't spend in a given week we put in a fund to be used for our vacation. We kicked in the creative juices on how to get more for our dollar when purchasing food. I will never forget how exciting it was when we ended up with $2,000 laid aside to use for fun when we went on our vacation." One of the purposes of money is to deepen the marital relationship and enrich the lives of our children. This couple had found that creative spending helped them do that.

PUTTING THE PRINCIPLES INTO PRACTICE

1. Would you be willing to sit down with your spouse, look at each of the ideas suggested in this chapter, and ask the question "Is this for us?" Here are the creative spending ideas covered in the chapter:

> Discount shopping
> Recycle shopping
> Free shopping
> Seasonal shopping

2. Does either of you have a skill, such as sewing or refurnishing furniture, that could be used to improve your family finances?

3. What additional creative ideas can you come up with related to spending or making things for yourselves that would enhance your family's financial condition?

7

*A*n old adage says, "Live within your means." To put it more pointedly, "Don't spend money that you don't have." It is a lesson that few couples in our society have learned. Consequently, many couples have found money to be a drain on their relationship.

The necessities are relatively few. I am certain they can be met on your present income. (If you are unemployed, then our government has help for you. The poorest in this country can have the necessities.) I am not opposed to aspiring for more than the necessities, but I am suggesting that you live in the present rather than the future. Leave the future joys for future accomplishments. Enjoy today what you have today.

Earlier in the book, I suggested setting the goal of giving away 10 percent of your income, saving 10 percent, and living on the remaining 80 percent. I suggested that goal because I believe it is a wise pattern of financial management. I suggested it also because I know it works. When my wife and I were first married, I was in graduate school. She was working part time, and I was working part time. Our income was meager, but our plan worked. During those years, we began to play a little game that we came to enjoy very much. It is called Let's See How Many Things We Can Do Without That Everyone Else Must Have. I don't remember where we got the idea, but very soon we were hooked on the game and continued to play it long after it was necessary.

The game works like this: On Friday night or Saturday, you go together to a department store and walk down the aisles, looking at whatever catches your eye. Read the labels, talk about how fascinating each item is, and then turn to each other and say, "Isn't it great that we don't have to have that?" Then while others walk out with arms loaded and names duly signed on charge slips, you walk out hand in hand, excited that you do not need "things" to be happy. I highly recommend this game for all young married couples.

USING CREDIT CARDS

I must admit it was much easier to play that game in those years than it is today because credit cards were not given as freely as they are now. I remember when we were getting ready for the arrival of our baby. We both agreed that we needed a crib, so we went to the local Sears store and applied for a credit card in order to buy one. However, our application was refused because of our low income. Had we received the card, we may well have been on our way to spending money that we did not have. Instead, because we were refused, we asked around and found a couple who were happy to loan us a crib that they were no longer using. Looking back, I've always been grateful to Sears for helping us live within our means.

Unfortunately, the department stores and credit-card companies in today's world have removed those standards, and anyone can get a credit card. In fact, the media screams from every corner: "Buy now! Pay later!" What is not stated is that if you buy now without cash, you will pay *much more* later. Interest rates on charge accounts are usually 18 to 21 percent, or even higher. Couples need to read the small print . . . and then read it again.

I am not opposed to having a credit card. In fact, in today's world, it is difficult to travel without one. You cannot rent a car with cash, and few people use cash to purchase airline tickets. The problem is not having the card; the problem is using the card to purchase what you cannot afford. For many couples, the credit card has been a membership card to "the society of the financially frustrated." It encourages impulse buying when most of us have more impulses than we can afford to follow. I know that credit cards can aid in keeping records and that, if payments are made promptly, charges are minimal. Most couples, however, will spend more and stretch out payments longer if they have credit cards. The business community's eagerness to issue credit cards is evidence of this fact.

Why do we use credit? Because we want now what we cannot pay for now. In the purchase of a house, using credit may be a wise financial move. We would have to pay rent anyway. If a house is well selected, it will appreciate in value. If we have money for the down payment and can afford the monthly payments, such a purchase is wise.

But the sad fact is that most of our purchases do not appreciate in value. On the contrary, their value begins to decrease the day we buy them. We buy them before we can afford them. Then, over a period of time, we pay the purchase price plus the interest charges while the articles themselves continue to depreciate in value. Why? For the momentary pleasure that the items bring. I ask, "Is this a sign of responsible money management?

WAITING UNTIL YOU HAVE THE FUNDS
Living within your means will require waiting. Rather than purchasing now and paying more later, we make a choice to wait until we have the money

to make the purchase. Many times when we follow this guideline, by the time we have the money, we realize that we no longer want the product. So we can use the money we have saved to purchase something that will benefit our relationship.

For most young couples, there is probably enough unused stuff in their parents' garage and grandmother's attic that they would not need to purchase anything for the first two years of marriage. And chances are, parents and grandparents would be glad for it to be used—in fact, would probably make a gift of it.

Waiting builds character. Patience is a virtue that is developed by waiting. In the process of waiting, we have an opportunity to evaluate the importance of a purchase and are far more likely to make wise purchases. Children also need to learn the virtue of waiting. When we fulfill every desire of children instantly, we set them up for failure as adults. Life is a process. We aspire to accomplish certain things in life, and we take the necessary steps to get there. Waiting to make purchases teaches us the art of responsible living.

Waiting stimulates our creativity. If we greatly desire something, we tend to be creative about ways to get the money to purchase it. One couple, who agreed that they really wanted to have a weekend away but knew that they could not afford it, sat down to think about what they might do to earn some extra money. The wife was an excellent cook and baked especially delicious pound cakes. They selected a restaurant that they knew did not have very good desserts. She donated one of her cakes to the restaurant as a "trial run." The restaurant had so many compliments that the owners agreed to start buying cakes from her. Before long, they also wanted pies. Within six months, the woman had to recruit one of her friends to help her make the desserts. Their homemade desserts developed into a very profitable part-time job for both of them. Not only did this couple's creative thinking provide them the funds for a weekend away, it also provided an ongoing stream of income they had not anticipated.

Waiting provides time for you to analyze what funds you are presently spending for activities or products that are not beneficial to your marriage or to your health. Upon reflection, one couple decided to stop drinking colas for three months. Another husband decided to give up cigarettes. Another couple decided to live without desserts for six months. Choosing to eliminate something from your normal list of purchases creates funds that can be applied to those things you deem to be valuable.

For many of us, living within our means will require that we lower our standard of living. It may mean returning to a smaller house and driving a preowned vehicle. It may mean purchasing used furniture rather than new. It may mean borrowing a crib rather than purchasing one. Our society has not trained us in the art of scaling back. Everyone encourages us to aspire for more, but the evidence is overwhelming that more does not always mean a better relationship. Most couples in this country could live on far less and would be far happier. Most of us are trying to "keep up with the Joneses," rather than demonstrating to the Joneses that a simpler life may well be a happier life.

Far too many couples get married and try to have in the first year of marriage what it took their parents thirty years to accumulate. Why must you have the biggest and best now? With such a philosophy, you destroy the joy of aspiration and attainment. When you acquire immediately, the joy is short lived and you spend months trying to pay for things. Why saddle yourself with such unnecessary pain?

Couples who live within their means create for themselves a world relatively free of financial stress and also teach their children many valuable lessons. They do not fear the creditor because they do not have a creditor. They are enjoying the profit-sharing plan of never spending money they don't have.

PUTTING THE PRINCIPLES INTO PRACTICE

1. Have you ever seriously considered giving 10 percent, saving 10 percent, and living on 80 percent of your income? Would this be a good time for the two of you to discuss this possibility?

2. Do you feel financially strapped? Do you have more bills than you can pay each

month? If so, would you be willing to consider some of the options discussed in this chapter, such as lowering your standard of living? What practical steps could you take to make this a reality?

3. Try playing the game Let's See How Many Things We Can Do Without That Everyone Else Must Have. This Friday or Saturday would be a good time to start.

4. Talk with your spouse about initiating the concept of waiting to make future purchases until you have the money in hand.

5. Are there creative things that either of you could do that might increase the flow of income for your budget?

8

*T*ogether, a husband and wife must develop a plan for handling their finances. The fact is, every couple needs a budget. Some couples, when they hear the word *budget,* go into trauma. One husband said, "Oh no. I don't want to get on one of those things. You can never be spontaneous, and you will always be counting every penny."

The fact is, you are already on a budget. A budget is simply a plan for handling your finances. You may never have written your plan on paper, but you have a plan. Some couples' plan is to spend all their money the day they get it. The stores stay open late now, and you can do that. Not a very good plan, but it is a plan. Other couples' plan is to spend all their money *before* they get it. So everything is purchased on credit cards, and they make the monthly payments according to what they have left over. These couples are headed for disaster. Other couples seek to be more responsible.

PUTTING YOUR BUDGET ON PAPER

If you have never put your budget on paper, it's a good idea to do so. But don't try to do it today. Instead, I suggest that you start by keeping records for two months. Record all the money that comes in, all the money you give away and what you give it to, the money you save, and the money you spend and what you spend it for. After two months, you will have your present budget. This is the plan you have been following without thinking. Now it's time to think.

Look at your budget and ask yourselves, "Is this the way we want to be handling our money? Do we want to give more? save more? Do we want to spend our money in a better way? How could we apply the principles in this book to either increase our income or become better managers of the money we spend?" Together, work out a budget that you both feel comfortable with, one that will alleviate stress if you follow it.

Let me also suggest that you include in your plan some money for each of you to use as you wish without accounting for every penny. This doesn't have to be a large amount, but a husband needs to be able to buy a candy bar without having to ask his wife for a dollar. Likewise, a wife needs to be able to go out to lunch with a friend without asking her husband for a loan. Whatever amount you decide on, it should be an equal amount for the husband and the wife. This is money with which each of you can buy incidentals for yourself and not feel you are violating the family budget.

CHOOSING A BOOKKEEPER

Once the two of you have agreed on a plan for allocating your money, then one of you must become the bookkeeper. Since you are a team, why not let the team member best qualified for the task take it on? As a couple discuss financial details, it will usually be obvious which one is more adept at such matters. Why not assign that one the responsibility?

This does not mean that the one chosen to keep the books is in charge of making financial decisions. Such decisions are to be made as a team. The bookkeeper is simply keeping the couple on track with their plan. He or she is paying the monthly bills, balancing the check register monthly, and seeing that the funds are spent according to the plan upon which both have agreed. It is a formidable task. But for one who enjoys working with numbers, it can be satisfying.

The bookkeeper may not necessarily remain the bookkeeper forever. For various reasons, you may agree that after the first six months, it would be far wiser if the other partner became the bookkeeper. It is your marriage, and you are responsible for making the most of your resources. However, be certain that the one who is not keeping the books knows how to do so and has full knowledge of the various checking and savings accounts. Let's be realistic. As much as we avoid thinking about it, the fact is that one of you will likely die before the other. A good working knowledge of the system you've been using will leave the surviving spouse much better equipped to take over the family finances. It will also be helpful if the spouse who normally does the bookkeeping becomes sick and is unable to fulfill those responsibilities for a time.

And making sure both of you have full knowledge of your financial affairs is also good for your marital relationship. When one spouse keeps the books and the other is uninformed, there can develop a parent-child mentality. When this happens, it is detrimental to the marriage relationship. You are partners; it is your shared money—but while one is keeping the books, the other needs to be fully informed and to feel comfortable with how the money is being used.

PUTTING THE PRINCIPLES INTO PRACTICE

1. There are three things we can do with money: Give it away, spend it, and save it. Does your budget include all these areas?

2. If you have never put your budget on paper, will you consider keeping records for two months to find out what your present budget really is?

3. After keeping records, would you be willing to sit down with your spouse to analyze your present plan and discuss changes that need to be made to move you in a more positive direction?

4. Who do you think is best qualified to keep the books in your marriage?

5. Does either of you feel that you are not an equal partner in the financial area of your marriage? If so, what steps need to be taken to change this perception?

In this brief book, I have shared with you eight key insights on how to make money an asset in your marriage.

- It all begins with attitude. Your relationship is more important than money. You are a team, and you need to work together in managing your money.

- Work is a noble endeavor. Work is God's plan, each couple providing for your own needs and the needs of your children.

- In God we trust. Money is to be your servant, never your master. You tell money what to do. Money does not tell you what to do.

- Giving is an expression of gratitude. All that you have is a gift from God. Out of gratitude, you may choose to give as you have received.

- Saving is a sign of wisdom. Saving is a responsible step in money management. Preparing for both a rainy day and a sunny vacation has merit.

- Creative spending enhances profit sharing. When you buy for less, you are increasing your income.

- Live within your means. Don't spend money that you don't have.

- Decide who will keep the books. But remember that the bookkeeper is not the boss. The bookkeeper simply follows the plan upon which both of you have agreed.

Having the right attitude toward your money and handling it as a responsible team will make money an asset to your relationship. Money should be managed in such a way that both of you feel loved, appreciated, and respected. What could be more important than that?

The size of the house, the model of the car, the price tags on the clothes are relatively unimportant. What is important is your relationship with each other and your relationship with God. Life's meaning is found not in money or the accumulation of things but in relationships: first of all, your relationship with God; second, your relationship as husband and wife; and last, your relationship with children, friends, church, and community.

When you use money to enhance relationships, you have found the purpose of money. Money then becomes an asset to your marriage, rather than a battleground upon which you shoot each other.

As husband and wife, you are on the same team. It is your money, and together you must find a way to manage it that allows both of you to be involved.

You must decide the sacrifices you will make, the goals you will establish, and the steps you will take to get there. When you work as a team, you are far more likely to accomplish your objectives. In the process, both of you will have opportunities to use your creativity for the benefit of the marriage.

If you remember that you are a team and, therefore, work as a team, seeking practical help where needed and agreeing on financial decisions, you will find money to be your faithful servant. If, however, you disregard the principles we have discussed in this book and simply "do what comes naturally," you will soon find yourself in the same financial crisis that has become a way of life to thousands of couples.

Some couples, because of poor models established by parents or lack of training by parents, have entered into marriage with very few money-management skills. Consequently, they soon find themselves in financial trouble. If you are one of these couples, I urge you to enroll in a class at your church on financial management, read a book on the topic, or go for private personal counseling.

Perhaps a combination of all three of these is the answer. Help is readily available. You do not need to continue in a state of financial crisis. The sooner you reach out for help, the sooner you will get on the road to financial stability. It will require honesty, openness, and a willingness to change. But together you can do it. And when you do, you will both participate in the profit-sharing plan and make money an asset to your marriage.

If you are presently feeling the pain of crisis, it is time for a radical change. There is a way out. If you cannot think clearly enough to solve the problem, then it is time to seek the counsel of a trusted friend or financial counselor who can help you take a realistic look at your situation and decide the steps that need to be taken to bring you to a healthier financial position. Do not continue to allow finances to cripple your marriage. Money was designed to be an asset to your relationship, not a divisive factor.

Learning to handle money in a responsible and mutually satisfying manner is a huge step in creating a healthy marriage. I hope that the ideas I have shared in this book will be helpful to you as you seek to grow in the skills of profit sharing. If you find this book helpful, I hope you will share it with a friend. If you have stories to share with me, I invite you to select the Contact link at www.garychapman.org.

Some Thoughts Worth Remembering

- Money can be used to provide more creature comforts, but money will not create a successful marriage. It is the pursuit of righteous living, love, patience, gentleness, and compassion that builds meaningful relationships.

- The desire to have more material possessions is not necessarily an evil desire. The problem comes when we allow money to become the focus of our lives.

- Some have implied that work was a part of the curse after Adam and Eve sinned. This was not the case; God instituted work before man's sin. Work is a gift of God.

- Any task can be done cheerfully and with pride—or grudgingly and with rebellion. The manner in which we do them is really up to us. It is a matter of choice. There are no menial jobs, only menial attitudes.

🌿 It is daily talking with God, seeking his wisdom and guidance, that makes us most productive financially as well as in all other areas of life.

🌿 The wise couple will make money their servant. They will seek to use money for the good of their family and to help others. They will never allow money to be their master, dictating their decisions.

🌿 There are only three things we can do with money. We can give it away, we can save it, or we can spend it. All three are valid ways of using money.

🌿 Obviously, we cannot and should not give all of our money away. Some must be used to meet the physical needs of our families. But if we give none of it away, we are failing to be grateful for what God has given us.

- Some feel that Christians should not save; that saving money is a sign that we are not trusting God to provide for the future. However, this is not the perspective found in Scripture. The Scriptures indicate that we are to be good managers of our money. The wise manager faces the future realistically.

- Many financial advisors suggest allotting 10 percent of your net income to savings. You may choose more or less; the choice is yours. However, if you save only what is left over at the end of the week or the month, you will not save. Being regular and consistent in what you save is more important than the amount you save.

- Creative spending can become an exciting part of life for the couple who are trying to take hold of their finances, utilize their assets in the best possible manner, and create money that can be used in other ways to enrich their marriage.

- Living within your means will require waiting. Rather than purchasing now and paying more later, we choose to wait until we have the money to make the purchase.

- Our society has not trained us in the art of scaling back. Everyone encourages us to aspire for more, but the evidence is overwhelming that more does not always mean a better relationship.

- A budget is simply a plan for handling your finances. You may never have written your plan on paper, but you have a plan.

- Let me suggest that you include in your plan some money for each of you to use as you wish without accounting for every penny. This doesn't have to be a large amount, but a husband needs to be able to buy a candy bar without having to ask his wife for a dollar. Likewise, a wife needs to be able to go out to lunch with a friend without asking her husband for a loan.

☙ Be certain that the one who is not keeping the books knows how to do so and has full knowledge about various checking and savings accounts.

Additional Resources

MONEY AND FINANCES
Crown Financial Ministries
P.O. Box 100
Gainesville, GA 30503-0100
Phone: 1-800-722-1976
Web site: www.crown.org

A wealth of resources covering all aspects of money management, including personal budget coaching, financial advice, seminars, workbooks, online articles, and an e-newsletter.

Larry Burkett, *The Complete Financial Guide for Young Couples: A Lifetime Approach to Spending, Saving, and Investing* (Chariot Victor Publishing, 1993)
This book covers establishing a workable budget, knowing how much insurance to purchase, recognizing economic dangers in a marriage, exploring investments, and teaching children about finances.

Howard Dayton, *Your Money Map: A Proven 7-Step Guide to True Financial Freedom* (Moody Publishers, 2006)
By revealing key biblical principles of finance through the journey of a married couple, Matt and Jennifer, *Your Money Map* steers you toward the clear biblical basics of money management and through seven financial "destinations" that anyone can reach.

Howard Dayton, *Your Money Counts: The Biblical Guide to Earning, Spending, Saving, Investing, Giving, and Getting Out of Debt* (Tyndale House Publishers, 1997)

In *Your Money Counts,* you will learn that the Bible has a lot to say about money. Indeed, the Bible is a blueprint for managing your finances. You will also discover the profound impact handling money has on your relationship with God.

CREATIVE SPENDING
Ellie Kay, *Half-Price Living: Secrets to Living Well on One Income* (Moody Publishers, 2007)

A recent online survey found that 86 percent of working moms said they would stay at home if they were financially able to do so. Popular author and speaker Ellie Kay used both her financial expertise and her experience as a mom to write this step-by-step plan on how to downsize from two incomes to one.

Margaret Feinberg, Jason Boyett, Katie Meier, and Josh Hatcher, *Cheap Ways to . . .* (Relevant Books, 2003)

The authors offer fun, innovative ideas designed to help you make your resources stretch a little further while avoiding or escaping the pitfalls of mass consumerism and credit-card debt.

LIVING WITHIN YOUR MEANS
Howard Dayton, *Free and Clear: God's Roadmap to Debt-Free Living* (Moody Publishers, 2006)

Becoming debt free may seem an impossible dream, but it is actually an attainable goal. Howard Dayton, past president of Crown Financial Ministries, overcame his own struggle with debt by applying God's principles to managing his finances, principles he lays out in this practical and encouraging book.

SAVING AND INVESTING
Austin Pryor, *The Sound Mind Investing Handbook: A Step-by-*

Step Guide to Managing Your Money from a Biblical Perspective
(**Sound Mind Investing, 2004**)
Investment advisor Austin Pryor has carefully created the "next step"
guide that helps you put godly principles of finance into motion.
Each user-friendly lesson is written in everyday English and filled
with helpful visual aids. You'll learn what investing is and why it's
actually quite simple, important steps to take to prepare yourself
financially before you invest, what mutual funds are and why they
make investing easier than ever before, and how to use your personal
investing temperament and present season of life to make decisions
and limit your risk.

Larry Burkett, Ron Blue, and Jeremy White, *The Burkett & Blue
Definitive Guide to Securing Wealth to Last: Money Essentials for
the Second Half of Life* (**B&H Publishing Group, 2003**)
In this book Ron Blue and the late Larry Burkett, primary trailblaz-
ers and leaders in Christian financial teaching, provide direction for
building a financial portfolio that will provide for your family and
help you to honor God.

Notes

CHAPTER 1

1. Luke 12:15.
2. 1 Timothy 6:10.

CHAPTER 2

1. Genesis 1:28.
2. Genesis 2:15.
3. Exodus 20:8-10.
4. William J. Bennett, *The Book of Virtues* (New York: Simon & Schuster, 1993), 347.
5. Proverbs 13:19.
6. As quoted in George Sweeting, *Who Said That?* (Chicago: Moody Publishers, 1995), 452.
7. 1 Timothy 5:8.
8. Proverbs 6:6-11.
9. Proverbs 13:4.
10. 2 Thessalonians 3:10-12.
11. Colossians 3:23-24.

CHAPTER 3

1. James 1:17.
2. C. S. Lewis, *Mere Christianity* (New York: McMillan, 1952), 180.
3. James 1:5.
4. R. G. LeTourneau, *Mover of Men and Mountains* (Chicago: Moody Publishers, 1972), 263.
5. Matthew 6:25-33.

6. Philippians 4:6-7.
7. Matthew 6:24.
8. Joshua 1:8-9.
9. Joshua 24:15.

CHAPTER 4
1. Leviticus 27:30-34.
2. Malachi 3:8-12.
3. Matthew 23:23.
4. Luke 6:38.
5. 2 Corinthians 9:6-8.
6. Proverbs 3:9-10.
7. Philippians 4:18-19.
8. R. G. LeTourneau, *Mover of Men and Mountains,* 280.
9. 1 John 3:17-18.

CHAPTER 5
1. Proverbs 22:3, TLB.
2. Luke 14:28-30.
3. Genesis 41:34-36.
4. Proverbs 21:20.
5. Proverbs 6:6-8.

About the Author

Dr. Gary Chapman is the author of the perennial best seller *The Five Love Languages* (more than 3.5 million copies sold) and numerous other marriage and family books. He is currently working with best-selling author Catherine Palmer on a new fiction series based on *The Four Seasons of Marriage;* the first book, *It Happens Every Spring,* is available in bookstores and online. Dr. Chapman is the director of Marriage and Family Life Consultants, Inc.; an internationally known speaker; and the host of *A Growing Marriage,* a syndicated radio program heard on more than 100 stations across North America. He and his wife, Karolyn, live in North Carolina.

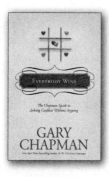